Tears on My Tongue

HAIKU JOURNAL for a Pandemic Year

Poems—Rob Godfrey

Version 1.0
August 1, 2023

ISBN: 979-8-218246-07-5

waynegoodmanbooks@gmail.com
Instagram: @waynegoodmanbooks

Print versions at independent booksellers
Electronic versions and Audiobooks
Available online

FOREWORD & DEDICATION:

Artful life seemed lost as the Covid pandemic unfolded in 2020. I wrote not one thing in 2020. Midst pandemic, 2021 began darkly, full of worry. Indoor musical performance was impossible, friends and family were falling ill; community activities, dining together, all forbidden. Politics? Toxic rhetoric from an earlier, uglier time. Light began to enter with the first vaccines in February. I was fortunate in my musical friends, who adapted during 2020 away from customary indoor sessions and performances to organize small groups playing in parks and backyards. As the light began to slowly grow, we discovered Farmer's Markets to share music—no matter the cold wind or scarcely-shaded sun, all year long. And I didn't get sick...My heartfelt thanks to Cata Fitzgerald, Robin Somerville, Barbara Judd, and Rodger Bickham of San Francisco Scottish Fiddlers for music in that dark time and straight on 'til morning.

This effort is a poet's diary of 2021 in the form of haiku. I dedicate the book to fellow poet John Campion, who offered the "2021 Haiku Challenge" to all the writers he knew and not a few additional artists in other media and widespread friends across the country. This is what he suggested:

"Haiku—one per week—nothing is expected"

Haiku...What are haiku? The most common form, counting syllables exactly as I have done in this volume, is not essential; but any chosen haiku form focusses the writer's attention and captivates the imagination. I enjoyed the common meter as a meditation, just as I enjoyed finding the images, feelings, words to express the moments that shaped each week of the year, sometimes moments from long ago and far away. This "Haiku Challenge" proved to be a rewarding exercise in thoughtful writing, and it helped immensely in capturing the joy that can be found in the darkest times. It was effectively therapeutic in turmoil and tumult...I'm saying that the challenge itself is the most important thing I have to share with you:

Nothing is expected!

Rob Godfrey
The Yellow House
Oakland, California
January, 2023

Thank you to the artist:

The cover is a still life captured by the artist Kenneth Cook just before the pandemic began in 2020. It makes me think of Pompeii, a fresco painted on the wall of home before the storm...just right.

Kenneth's work can be viewed at his website kencookartist.com

–Rob Godfrey

EACH WEEK ENDS *on* FRIDAY

January 1: 1

Icicle melting
tears on my tongue taste of dust
sunblades bright, blinding

January 8: 2

Saturn, Jupiter
owls in the evening sky
winged planets soar

January 15: 3

Our world cries aloud
my violin lightly held
vibrates harmony

January 22: 4

Melody my soul
rhythm metering my life
others harmony

January 29: 5

Glinting tesserae
mosaic faces, our dreams
new constellations

February 5: 6

Once foetal daughter
trimester somersault glee
now her own child spins

February 12: 7

...the name of my touring bike

Gullinbursti bears
Freyr, the god, joyful peddling
weekend fiddle rides

February 19: 8

...but with a plan, and it was time

Houseroom forsaking

embracing the pestilence

bitter friend fares forth

February 26: 9

500,000

mind refuses to accept

day dawns over death

March 5: 10

Under forest boughs
Red Efts heave from winter mulch
strive toward the lake

March 5: 11

Looking back, Red Efts
dry skin, rimmed spots, eyes agleam
'neath leaves, orange coals

March 12: 12

Oh no, you bit me!
the glad cormorants batten
feathered seals on fry

March 12: 13

Unsafe, unsettled
shuttling worlds weave darkness
a cloak rent by stars

March 19: 14

Hear the Crack of Noon
a knell shakes thy byre: Awake!
fair evening's prize

March 19: 14

Migration windrow
Cedar Waxwings huddle close
rest on rain-washed tree

March 19: 14

Dangerous conceit:
wear that lucky pair of socks
in spots they grow holes

March 26: 17

Hearing rainfall peen
pebbled course below the eaves
Spring answers Winter

March 26: 18

First warm days of Spring and
friends to share adventure year
of darkness fades

April 2: 19

Hinny queens dream of flight
glad beekeepers capture swarms
hiving the hiveless

April 9: 20

California
newts rut, roiling in spring dance
vernal pool asquirm

April 16: 21

Joyful among friends
pint after pint, the glad ale
rain on yearning fields

April 23: 22

Bare room resonates
old fir floor, spruce-top fiddle
singing together

April 23: 22

...remembering Desmond Rutherford...dramatically

Farewell to Desmond
long-wish'd memorial hoot
new fiddle neck crack'd

April 30: 24

Sunlight scintillant
shingly sea-merge streambed
dream whales ripple waves

April 30: 25

Now on sunny days
jaywalking geriatrics
smile, wave, say hello

May 7: 26

Dancing with despair
glad memories suppressed, gone
world weeps species death

May 14: 27

Reaching for right tool
repairs in hand, shaped ideas
sunlit garden glows

May 21: 28

Sun setting like blood
oil on spindrift-tossing seas
human hearts grasp peace

May 28: 29

Under drifted leaves
deep, dusty, filtering light
scent of Autumn peace

May 28: 30

Violent struggle
weasel and blacksnake wrestle
seen, submerged in leaves

May 28: 31

Deep beneath piled leaves
damp pages in unread books
worms, pill bugs, dream Spring

June 4: 32

Words wriggling, alive
poets winkling trout in heaven
weirs along the river

June 4: 33

Under lake, Winter
frogs sleep in warm rotting leaves
dipnet miracle

June 4: 34

Fallen years, layered
oldest moist with corruption
teeming with new life

June 4: 35

Oakleaf drey, soft creche
squirrel kits squirm, eyes open
glimpse tree-fingered dawn

June 4: 36

Love strong, sharp winds shape
another year of wonder
Cathy-month concludes

June 11: 37

Kayak surges swift
tide races for, against: Wind
rustles silent bay

June 11: 38

Fleets of pelicans
drive fat fish, Morro Bay delight
pods guzzle finned prey

June 11: 38

Pelagic corm'rant
red-leg momma penguins down
ledge-way to sea cave

June 18: 40

Eight weeks 'til Susie!
Jessie's aqueous orb glows
sonar face dream smiles

June 25: 41

...Happy Vax, masks Relax

Proud gorgets dangling
string chains, un-silvered badges
masks have done duty

July 2: 42

... Road Trip! Nevada highway

Mormon crickets piled
hubris paid in death
black snow, roadside drifts

July 2: 43

... Road Trip! Outside Elko

Mountain hyssop breath
aspen boughs swaying
night fills glacial bowl

July 2: 44

... Road Trip! Moscow Arboretum 110 °F

Green Evening stroll
cool sprays bathe crab-apples
bathe robins, bathe us

July 2: 45

... Road Trip! Columbia Gorge

One-hundred nineteen!
Maryhill Stonehenge blasted
white peacocks no more

July 9: 46

...Boundary Waters Adventures!

Minnesota lakes

pristine waters, light canoes

wilderness joy heals

July 9: 47

...Boundary Waters Adventures!

Merganser, an ark
row'd chicks, stegosaurus plates
one falls off, swims fast

July 9: 48

...Boundary Waters Adventures!

Light, morning air
final cry of loon echoes
pristine lakes abide

July 16: 49

Shared music anew
gift of reopening world
players' joyful song

July 16: 50

Unseen friends gather
twelve-month absence: twelve-year toll
single-malt tuns tapp'd

July 23: 51

Lucid dreaming worlds
life in the limitless now
all real, and nothing

July 23: 52

Malleting footsteps
unheard heartbeats; silent birds
unaugmented peace

July 30: 53

Floured wood surface
folded dough, round, refolded
oven baked scones, hot

July 30: 54

Ripe blackberry time
blood, bramble scratch, purple stains
high summer harvest

July 30: 55

Cool breezes of home
bayside protective embrace
fires threaten outlands

August 6: 56

...Welcome Susie!

Dawn, sun parting mists
water breaks, babe wriggles outward
new day, infant crowns

August 6: 57

...and Welcome Susie!

Artful wrigg'ler squirms
newborn planet joins orbit
Susie stretches, yawns

August 6: 58

...and Welcome Susie!

Jessie, jaundiced lay
clasp'd my finger in her fist
years ago; yesterday

August 6: 59

...and Welcome Susie!

Dad's nightlong vigil
knight forged; rocking infant
parents forged, and love

August 6: 60

...and Welcome Susie!

Never forgotten friends: Jessie and Evelyn doula delivers!

August 13: 61

Zoetrope year turns
lit by flame, images spin
flowers in the night

August 13: 62

Wall of falling waves
pelicans sail in silence
layered sea, flight, sky

August 13: 63

...my cousin Drew Huffman

Missing Drew tonight

family in Seattle

stories, drawing close

August 13: 64

Memories like leaves
swarming trunks to hang from twigs
family minds past

August 20: 65

...bike ride Oakland to Davis

Sleeping under stars

stiff zephyrs scour Delta skies

moonrise silent song

August 20: 66

...a long ride ahead

Orion, blind side
riding River Road pre-dawn
Jupiter ahead

August 20: 67

...California fires

60's, smog like smoke
shameful stain, the world in pain
smoke like smog, too late

August 27: 68

Unvisited friends
unfinished books, ravelled ends
turbid minds encyst

September 3: 69

...Suzanne Gowman 9/3/32

Mother, a stranger

moment for understanding

lost to time, but love

September 10: 70

Singing to strangers
a lens drawing light to share
footlight diffraction

September 10: 71

Playing over Zoom
impossible barrier
unlaupt prison wall

September 10: 72

But walls between us
diaphanous film to part
no void between worlds

September 10: 73

Dappled forest marge
transitional world, no wall
sunlight bathes cradle

September 10: 74

Horizons recede
you are just beyond my reach
branches extend leaves

September 17: 75

Musters to murders
rattles and caws, roost and flight
our town rings with crows

September 24: 76

Squinting moon-bathers
heather shadows; out-stretch'd limbs
auspicious nimbus

October 1: 77

Feather'd mercury
childhood's crushed thermometers
sacred pool: dust sport

October 8: 78

Sole undamaged eye
equates the eagle, the seagull
size, not cries, not shapes

October 8: 79

Welling, swelling night
soul and body defend mind
La Brea attacks

October 8: 80

Holding the last note
brief beauty graves the moment
sunset yields to night

October 8: 81

Body, mind unique
world around, river beyond
our common soul sings

October 8: 82

Three poets unfolding
striding sunstruck sky
sowing, singing, each

October 15: 83

Frog's eye, a jewel
behold his legs in motion
at rest, life pulsing

October 22: 84

... Òran son Ròin a Thàladh

Singing of the seals
calls me to the rocks, the sea
I sing back; transform

October 22: 85

Toggles at my breast
webbed fingers and fused shinbones
selkie suit tight: Swim!

October 29: 86

...the name of my bike; Freyr's pig...

Gullinbursti breasts
wind and rain, song-brakes squealing
through storm-swept Oakland

October 29: 87

Missing Stonehenge pales
sunk below, eroded, gone
time-pierced ectoderm

November 5: 88

...Masks far and away...

Always in Venice

gala anonymity

bright-painted paste masks

November 5: 89

...Covid masks

Cloth and fiber
woven prophylactics
hard to celebrate

November 5: 90

...Venice masks

Decorate the eyes
hide the forehead; free the smile
allow the voice, song

November 5: 91

...Covid masks in contrast

Hide the mouth, lose all
expression, voice, shared feeling
speaking eyes not enough

November 5: 92

...Yet even masks of Venice...

Horrid Plague Doctors
nosegays, no visible mouth
stalk Venice like Death

November 12: 93

Moon's ecliptic line
Jove, Saturn, Venus in flames
fishing tomorrow

November 12: 94

Sun fallen darkness
horizon, surface of pool
sunken Mars swims deep

November 19: 95

Point Isabel Park
Daffy swam the Hellespont
each time, best of dogs

November 19: 96

Stillness, breath, a thought
potent note in any song
silence begins all

November 19: 97

World-ocean, ceaseless
welling drone, skirls of warpipes
life in fear, silent

November 19: 98

Thought, reaching out
timeless silence, creation
bathes in dank pool

November 26: 99

Spine bears open book
stiff breeze riffles printed leaves
recitation still

December 3: 100

Maryland winter
persimmons ripe after freeze
gold leaves, wild boy, deer

December 10: 101

Wading through tadpoles
cattails and blackbirds, toads teem
ice-pond nursery

December 10: 102

Under garden stones
Dekay snakes of Baltimore
cool lives in warm hands

December 10: 103

Brambles, raspberries
box turtles roam sunlit halls
eyes like hawks, beaks snap

December 17: 104

...John Campion day

Mayan mysteries
gods too drink wine from strange cups
quaff John's birthday toast

December 24: 105

Blocks of rain tumble
swept tiles fashion windrow walls
grey skies bleakly lour

December 24: 106

Long days, sweltering
boyhood summers, but blacksnakes
throat-wrapped, cool, refresh

December 24: 107

Shuttles shape new tales
woven light across the naught
between threads dark waits

December 31: 108

Burnt sensors whining
debriding aids less than joy
heart more than strength

December 31: 109

Hike through snowy wood
boughs heavy, trail compact, sing
Tahoe sunset awes

December 31: 110

Reach for adventure
wonder small, wonder large, feel
snowfall silent, deep